MOTHER TERESA

MOTHER TERESA
A Life in Pictures

Roger Royle

Original Photography by Gary Woods

BCA

LONDON · NEW YORK · SYDNEY · TORONTO

A LABYRINTH BOOK

This edition published 1992 by BCA by arrangement with
Bloomsbury Publishing Limited, 2 Soho Square, London W1V 5DE

A CIP catalogue record for this book
is available from the British Library

CN 9250

10   9   8   7   6   5   4   3   2   1

MOTHER TERESA: A LIFE IN PICTURES
was produced by Labyrinth Publishing (UK) Limited

Art direction and design by Magda Valine
Typeset by Dorchester Typesetting Group Limited, Dorchester, UK
Printed and bound by Mohndruck Gmbh, Gütersloh, Germany

To Hilary Hunt, Ian Everall and Philippe Savoy, whose quality of friendship has been of tremendous value to me.

And to the students of Lord Mayor Treloar College, whose courage I greatly respect.

Facing challenges has always been part of Mother Teresa's life. As a young girl, contemplating whether she was really being called by God to enter a religious community, she was told by her mother, Drana, *"My daughter, if you begin something, begin·it wholeheartedly. Otherwise don't begin it at all."* [1] But at that time no one would ever have thought that she was about to embark on a life that was to be both an inspiration and a challenge for human beings whether they accepted her belief in God or not.

In fact, if we simply take the somewhat delicate appearance of Mother Teresa as a guide, we probably would have some difficulty in realizing the incredible force, strength and courage of this extraordinary individual. Her absolute determination to deal with almost impossible situations, her unstoppable energy and her complete devotion place her in an unique position within the world.

"It will be for posterity to decide whether she is a saint. I can only say that in a dark time she is a burning and a shining light; in a cruel time, a living embodiment of Christ's gospel of love; in a Godless time, the Word dwelling among us, full of grace and truth." [2]

This was the reaction of the celebrated author and broadcaster Malcolm Muggeridge after he had spent time writing about and talking with Mother Teresa. At the time he was not a man of conventional faith. He was often highly critical of the Church as an establishment, but this small, seemingly fragile woman spoke more to him of God's love than any number of sermons preached by the most eminent Christians from the most prestigious pulpits. And it is not difficult to see why.

Born on August 26, 1910 to Albanian parents, Nikola and Drana Bojaxhiu, Agnes Gonxha, who would one day become the celebrated Mother Teresa, was the youngest of three children. She grew up in the Yugoslavian town of Skopje, which was then part of Serbia. Then, as now, it was a troubled part of the world. That very year saw the first Albanian rising. Within two years the first Balkan War had broken out, and in 1914 Europe was facing the tension of World War I, one of the causes of which was the unrest in the Balkan States.

The Bojaxhiu family were very much caught up in this turmoil. Being Albanians living in Serbia, they could not possibly be unaffected. But as a family they were financially and lovingly secure.

In no way was poverty part of Agnes Gonxha's early life.

Her father was a prosperous merchant who traveled Europe selling a wide range of luxury goods. When he returned home, he brought with him eagerly awaited presents for the family and very much enjoyed tales of his travels. But he was a disciplinarian. Agnes, her sister Aga, and her brother Lazar were expected to do as they were told. *"Never forget whose children you are!"* was Nikola's constant reminder to his offspring.

All three children went to an elementary school which was attached to their local church. From there the two sisters were sent to the Skopje Gymnasium, the state secondary school.

By all accounts they were both fine students, although Aga was possibly the more outstanding scholar. But Agnes Gonxha was always sensible, tidy, and well organized. They shared one another's love of music, especially singing, not just in the church choir but also with the Albanian Catholic Choir. Their brother, Lazar, left home in 1924 to attend a military school in Austria. His hobbies were sports so he spent most of his free time outside with young men his own age.

Their mother, Drana, was the daughter of a merchant and a landowner. Like her husband she was enterprising and hardworking. And it was a good thing, because when Agnes was only eight years old Nikola suddenly died, and Drana had the sole responsibility for the upbringing of the family. She set up a business selling handcrafted embroidery, which later developed to include the locally crafted carpets for which Skopje was famous. She raised her children to be aware of others, especially those less fortunate than themselves. Mother Teresa has recalled, *"Many of the poor in and around Skopje knew our house, and none left it emptyhanded. We had guests at table every day. At first I used to ask, 'Who are they?' and Mother would answer, 'Some are relatives, but all of them are our people.' When I was older, I realized that the strangers were poor people who had nothing and whom my mother was feeding."*[3]

As well as teaching the children to be aware of the needs of others, Drana (or Nana Loke, Mother of my Soul, as the children called her) also impressed upon them that waste of any kind was unacceptable. One evening when the three children were being silly in their talk and their behavior, Drana, who had been listening to this idle banter, got up and left the room, switching

off the lights at the same time. As she left she told her children that there was no point in wasting electricity so that such foolishness could go on.

Drana drew tremendous strength from her Christian faith, both for herself and her family. Every evening the whole family would gather in the living room to recite the rosary. They belonged to the parish of the Sacred Heart, a parish consisting mainly of Albanians. Being a very small minority of the population of Skopje, they looked to their church for more than religious observance. It was also the social center of their lives, keeping alive their national traditions and identity. To the parish came a priest who was to have a great influence on Agnes Gonxha: Father Jambrenkovic of the Society of Jesus. For the youth of the parish he introduced a young people's society called the Sodality of the Blessed Virgin Mary. Membership of this society was to play a very important part in Agnes Gonxha's formative years. It was a society founded in 1563 that faced its members with the challenge of answering St. Ignatius Loyola's questions, *"What have I done for Christ? What am I doing for Christ? What will I do for Christ?"* For a person of Agnes Gonxha's sensitivity, this was a challenge that could not be ignored.

Along with that challenge, members of the Sodality took a great interest in the lives of saints and missionaries. Father Jambrenkovic had great enthusiasm for the missionary work of the Jesuits and was more than prepared to share his enthusiasm with his young parishioners. He regularly preached about the work of the mission field, and especially about the work that was done among the poor and the lepers. Father Jambrenkovic told them stories about, and read them letters from, priests who had gone from Yugoslavia to Bengal in 1924. These missionaries were stationed on the outskirts of Calcutta and the Sunderbans, a forest where the Ganges meets the sea. To young ears the lives of these missionaries sounded exotic, fascinating, and challenging, so naturally the appetites of his young listeners were whetted. Agnes Gonxha was certainly interested in what she heard. She helped Father Jambrenkovic to describe mission activities to the local people, drawing on a world map that showed all existing missions at that time. She suggested to her cousin that the money he was given for teaching students the mandolin could be given through her for the missions

in India. She was also part of a small prayer group whose intention it was to pray specifically for the missionary work of the Church.

Agnes Gonxha's spiritual development was also powerfully influenced by her visits to Letnice. Drana made regular pilgrimages to the shrine of Our Lady of Cernagore in Letnice and encouraged her daughters to do the same. Set in the mountains of Montenegro, this shrine provided physical as well as spiritual refreshment for the young Agnes Gonxha. She was a frail child, susceptible to malaria and whooping cough, and her mother thought the mountain air was good for her. But Agnes Gonxha was always losing herself in a book, so her sister Aga was given strict instructions to take her on long walks and to see that she had adequate rest. The times she spent at Letnice proved to be among the happiest of her childhood.

She went there for the last time on the feast of the Assumption of the Virgin in 1928, but it had been her regular visits to the shrine that had helped

Agnes Gonxha understand her vocation to serve God with her whole life. Although, as she said herself, her first desire to belong completely to God came to her when she was twelve years old, she spent six years struggling with this desire. There were times when she wondered whether she had a vocation at all and how she would know if she did. Father Jambrenkovic advised her that the only way she could be sure she had a vocation was the way in which she experienced the sense of joy. He explained that when you think God is calling you, you should feel joy in the contemplation of serving God and your neighbor. A deep joy should be the compass which gives direction to the choice of a life's vocation.

The compass was to point east. Leaving her family was not easy but Agnes Gonxha knew she had to if she was to respond to God's call not just to be a nun, but also to be a missionary. From all that she had heard and read her heart was set on India. Her mother found the news hard to take. She shut herself in her room and didn't reappear for twenty-four hours. But she knew that her wishes should always take second place to God's call, and she gave her daughter advice that has remained with her forever. *"Put your hand in His – in His hand – and walk all the way with Him."*[4]

Agnes Gonxha applied to join the Order of Loreto Nuns, whose missionaries were working in Bengal, but whose Mother House was in Dublin. Having been accepted, she left Skopje on September 25, 1928. She stayed in Zagreb waiting for the arrival of another, Betike Kanjc, who was also to join the Order. When Betike arrived, Agnes Gonxha, having said her final goodbyes to her family, started the difficult journey to Dublin with her. On their arrival they were met by the Mother Superior and two sisters of the Loreto nuns.

Agnes Gonxha spent only six weeks in the novitiate, during which time she studied English and learned something of the Order of which she was now a part. The Loreto Sisters are the Irish branch of the Institute of the Blessed Virgin Mary, which was founded in 1609 by a woman from Yorkshire, England, Mary Ward. Ward had gone to Flanders because of the persecution of English Catholics. Emigration was her only chance of following her vocation. But she also requested exemption from enclosure, because she wanted to be of maximum use to the poor who needed help. Mary Ward's dream was inscribed over her grave, *"To love the poor, persevere in the same, live, die and rise with them, was all the aim of Mary Ward."* After a fairly chequered history, the Order was strong enough in 1841 to respond to the request to establish a foundation in Calcutta.

On January 6, 1929 the Feast of the Epiphany, Agnes Gonxha arrived in Calcutta, but for her training as a novice with the Sisters of Loreto she was sent 450 miles north to the town of Darjeeling. Set in the foothills of the Himalayan range and surrounded by tea plantations on all sides, Darjeeling served as the summer capital for the British during the period when Calcutta was the capital of India. Darjeeling had been a very popular hill station since the British established it as a rest and recreation area for its troops in the mid 1800s. In 1828 two British officers spent some time in Darjeeling, or as it was then known, Dorje Ling, Place of Thunderbolts. They quickly appreciated its value as a site for a sanatorium and a hill station. Having managed to persuade the local king to grant them the site for a reasonable rent, the British began developing the area. Development was rapid. By 1840 a road had been constructed, numerous houses and a sanatorium built, and a hotel opened. It was another forty years or so before the famous miniature railway was constructed. By 1857 Darjeeling had a population of some 10,000.

In his book *India Britannica*[5] Geoffrey Moorhouse describes how there was a time when every hill station was like a home from home to which white people could go for three or four months and pretend that India had receded from their lives. Waited on hand and foot the British lived in elegance and style, far removed from the poverty, disease, and dirt of the city.

The life of a young novice was far from luxurious. According to one of Agnes Gonxha's contemporaries, *"Life in the novitiate in the 1930s was very different from what we have today. The novice mistress trained us in everything, and this she did in great detail. We went weekly to our confessor. For two hours a day, from nine to eleven in the morning, we taught little boys and girls in St. Teresa's school. It was a one-roomed school, and there were generally about twenty boys and girls from the families who lived around us on the hillside. I found Mother Teresa a very simple type of person. We never had any idea that she would ever leave Loreto. She was a sincere, religious type of novice."*[6]

On May 24, 1931 Agnes Gonxha took her first vows of poverty, chastity and obedience as a Sister of Loreto. She adopted Thérèse as her religious name after her patron saint, St. Thérèse of Lisieux or as she is often known, St. Thérèse of the Child Jesus. She had to adopt the Spanish spelling of the name as there was already a Thérèse who was a novice in Loreto.

St. Thérèse had died at the early age of twenty-four from tuberculosis, but her love for missions and her prayers for priests, especially missionaries, moved the Pope in 1927 to name her, along with St. Francis Xavier, patron of the missions of the world. By choosing her name, Sister Teresa was obviously accepting St. Thérèse's philosophy of life which can be summed up in these words: *"My little way,"* wrote St. Thérèse, *"is the way of spiritual childhood, the way of trust and absolute self surrender."*[7]

On May 14, 1937 Sister Teresa took lifetime vows of poverty, chastity, and obedience as a Loreto Sister in Darjeeling. She was now a professed nun. When her time in Darjeeling came to an end, Sister Teresa's superiors sent her to Calcutta, where the Loreto Sisters had a large property in the district of Entally on the eastern side of the city. It was a very depressed area in what had become a

rather depressed city. Behind a solid wall, within a large compound, the Loreto Sisters ran a school for about 500 students, known as Loreto Entally. They were mostly boarders and came from families who could afford the fees. Within the same compound there was another school, St. Mary's. This was a smaller school, and here the girls came from a wider variety of backgrounds. Lessons were taught in Bengali, yet another tongue for Sister Teresa to master. But master it she did, along with Hindi. Fluent also in English, she became a teacher of geography and later history. Teaching in both schools as well as giving full commitment to the daily religious life of the community meant Sister Teresa's schedule was demanding.

Mother Teresa also taught at the church school of St. Teresa. To get to this school she had to leave the ordered, quiet life of the walled convent and walk through the city streets of Calcutta. For the young Sister Teresa, the contrast must have been overwhelming. Leaving the cleanliness and peace of the convent, she passed through the noise, filth, suffering, and squalor of those who lived in the nearby slums. Here was human life, often at its weakest, packed together. Disease was rampant and the smell all-pervading. David Porter quotes

Sister Teresa as saying, *"When I first saw where the children slept and ate, I was full of anguish. It is not possible to find worse poverty. And yet they are happy. Blessed childhood! Though when we first met, they were not at all joyful. They began to leap and sing only when I had put my hand on each dirty head. From that day onwards they called me 'Ma,' which means 'Mother.' How little it takes, to make simple souls happy!"*[8]

On top of the school work she was also put in charge of the Daughters of St. Anne, a diocesan order of Bengali woman. Her only break in the year was an annual retreat for deepening her religious commitment.

Here in Calcutta, there was one very strong link with Skopje. The Sodality of the Blessed Virgin, which had so influenced Sister Teresa's early years, was active in St. Mary's school. Under the direction of Father Julien Henry, the priest of the local church, St. Teresa's, the young girls were helped in their desire to bring relief to the families who lived in utter poverty on the other side of the wall from St Mary's. Every Saturday some students visited many of these families while others tried to bring comfort to the poor and sick in the large Nilratan Sarkar Hospital. But however much she may have wanted to, Sister Teresa was not allowed to go with them. Obedient to the rule of her order, she stayed enclosed within the compound's walls.

It was on a train journey on September 10, 1946 that she felt that God was wanting to redirect her life. She received what has been described as "the call within a call."

"I was going to Darjeeling to make my retreat," recalls Mother Teresa. *"It was on that train that I heard the call to give up all and follow Him into the slums – to serve Him in the poorest of the poor. I knew it was His will and I had to follow Him. There was no doubt it was to be His work."*[9] As she explained later, *"The message was quite clear. I was to leave the convent and work with the poor while living among them. It was an order. I knew where I belonged, but I did not know how to get there."*[10]

When she returned to Calcutta a month later, the same determined faith that brought her to India in the first place drove her to get the permission she needed to fulfil her newfound calling. Sister Teresa shared her thoughts with other members of her Order. She also lost no time in seeking the support of her superiors, including the Archbishop of Calcutta. He listened with caution to her story.

Without revealing her identity, the Archbishop consulted Father Henry and her spiritual director Father Celeste Van Exem.

The relationship between a spiritual director and a nun is always a special one. Father Van Exem played an extremely important part in the spiritual life of the young Sister Teresa. He was one of the first to know about her "call within the call." He guided her through all her dealings with the Archbishop, and it was from him that she received the news that the permission she had prayed for had been granted. It was significant that it was Father Van Exem whom Sister Teresa asked to bless a sari, the typical sari of a poor Bengali woman, a small cross and a rosary. These were the signs and the symbols that Sister Teresa chose for the work that lay ahead.

There was no doubt that work was necessary. India was in a state of turmoil. As Eileen Egan describes in her book *Such a Vision of the Street,* "*1947 was the year when India entered into freedom, when, with the partition of the subcontinent into Pakistan and India, newly made borders were bathed in a sea of blood. . . . With partition, came one of the largest movements of population in history.*

As many as sixteen million men, women, and children were displaced, the Hindus and Sikhs fleeing into India and the Muslims into the two wings of the newly created Pakistan."[11] The struggle towards freedom was not easy. Under the leadership of Gandhi, nonviolent resistance grew and was even intensified when, as part of the British Empire, India was drawn into World War II. Boats that had been used to transport rice were requisitioned for the purposes of war. And in 1943 at least two million people lost their lives in one of India's most destructive famines.

August 16, 1946 saw yet more suffering in Calcutta. The Muslim League declared the day a "Direct Action Day." Three days before it took place the Muslim leader of the administration of Calcutta declared it a public holiday. Tension was great between Muslims and Hindus, and on that particular day tension boiled over into hatred and violence. The city was brought to a standstill. As Sister Teresa herself said, *"Then I saw bodies on the street, stabbed, beaten, lying there in dried blood."*[12] Calcutta also became home for many displaced people, and Sister Teresa was only too aware of their needs.

At first the Archbishop suggested that she work with the Daughters of St. Anne, who were already doing many of the things that Sister Teresa intended to do. But she felt that was not possible. After a day's work among the poor, the Daughters of St. Anne withdrew to their convent behind the high walls of the Entally compound. Sister Teresa's calling was to live among the poor and to share their lives.

Having established that no one else was doing similar work, Sister Teresa was told to write to the Mother General of Loreto in Dublin to get permission to be released from the congregation. There appears to be some confusion as to what actually happened. Apparently the Archbishop insisted that Sister Teresa asked for "secularization" which would have meant that she returned to being a lay woman, rather than "exclaustration," which meant that she would be able to leave a fairly enclosed Order, but still be bound by her vows of poverty, chastity, and obedience. Had she been granted "secularization" Sister Teresa would have found it very difficult to get others to join her to form a new religious community. Father Van Exem remonstrated with the Archbishop but to no avail. *"She must trust God fully,"* was his reply. However, when the reply came

from the Mother General, she gave Sister Teresa the permission she wanted. Sister Teresa was allowed to write to Rome and ask for an "indult of exclaustration." This didn't satisfy the Archbishop, who once again insisted that when she wrote to Rome she should ask for "secularization."

Rome doesn't rush these decisions, and for Sister Teresa the wait seemed endless. Eventually Pope Pius XII gave his permission on April 12, 1948 although the letter didn't arrive in Calcutta until August 7. She was given what she had prayed for rather than what the Archbishop had insisted she asked for. She was allowed to leave the Loreto Order, but she had to remain faithful to her vows of poverty, chastity, and obedience. And she now owed that obedience to the Archbishop of Calcutta and not the Loreto Order. But leaving the Order wasn't easy. She has asserted on many occasions that leaving Loreto was the most difficult step of her whole life, and the greatest sacrifice. As Sister Teresa said, *"Loreto meant everything to me."*[13] When the news that she was to leave the Order reached the ears of the other nuns, they were asked neither to criticize nor praise the action, but to pray for their companion.

Having laid aside her habit of the Loreto Order, she put on a simple sari and plain sandals and left for Patna, an ancient city on the Ganges, some 240 miles from Calcutta. It was also the home of the Medical Mission Sisters. Sister Teresa realized that if she was to be of any practical help to "the poorest of the poor" it was vital that she had some medical knowledge. At the Holy Family Hospital, which was staffed by Sisters, she learnt such basic skills as how to make a hospital bed, and to give injections and medicines. After some time observing, she was even able to help with the deliveries of babies. But in her conversation with the Sisters she always emphasized the spirituality of her future life, the hours of prayer, penance, and fasting. However it was pointed out clearly to her that if she was going to work with the poor, it was essential that she looked after herself. A good balanced diet, adequate rest, and personal hygiene would need to be part of her disciplined life. The Sisters made clear that her idea to "eat as little as the poor" was not very practical, if she was also going to work for their well-being.

When Sister Teresa returned to Calcutta after spending about three months with the Medical Mission Sisters in Patna, she went to live with the Little Sisters of the Poor at the house they ran for the elderly, St. Joseph's Home. She spent time caring for the elderly as well as visiting the poor in Moti Jihl, the "bustee" or old workers' housing which was just outside the convent walls in Entally. The work was not easy, and it was certainly lonely. But then as she wrote, *"God wants me to be a lonely nun laden with the poverty of the cross. Today I learned a good lesson. The poverty of the poor is so hard. When I was going and going till my legs and arms were paining, I was thinking how they have to suffer to get food and shelter. Then the comfort of Loreto came to tempt me, but of my own free choice, my God, and out of love for you, I desire to remain and do whatever is your holy will in my regard. Give me courage now, this moment."* [14] It appears that although Sister Teresa was willing to face up to the demands of God, she was certainly prepared to make demands of Him.

The time was coming for Sister Teresa to find somewhere of her own from which she could start her work. She had a word with Father Van Exem and he raised the matter with Michael Gomes, a member of a Bengali Catholic family. He had a large three-story colonial house, 14 Creek Street, which was half empty. The story goes that Michael's young daughter, Mabel, on hearing the request said, *"Father, the whole of the upstairs is empty, it is not being used; she could come to us."*[15]

In February 1949 Sister Teresa moved in, bringing with her a small suitcase. The room was furnished with a single chair, a packing case that served as a desk, and some extra wooden boxes that could serve as seats. With her came Charur Ma who had been the cook at St. Mary's Entally. Together they shopped for the supplies they needed for the "bustee" school, and Michael went with her, whenever he could, to beg for the medicines that the poor could in no way afford.

Soon people started to come to 14 Creek Street wishing to join Sister Teresa in her work. On March 19, 1949 Subashini Das, who had been a boarder at St. Mary's since she was nine years old, appeared asking whether she could join her in the work in the Calcutta slums. A few weeks later they were joined by

another former student, Magdalena Gomes. A few months later the numbers had grown to ten, but two early candidates decided to leave after testing their vocation. Every day the women, dressed in saris, went out to the poorest parts of the city seeking out for special care young children for whom life held little hope and people of all ages who were dying without care in the alleys, the gutters, and the crowded streets.

A year had passed since Sister Teresa had been given permission to leave Loreto, and now this permission was up for review. During the year Sister Teresa had taken out Indian citizenship. Certainly she had no wish to leave. And the Archbishop of Calcutta to whom she owed her oath of obedience decided that the time had come to put things on a firmer and more official footing. The Archbishop indicated his willingness to take steps to have Sister Teresa and her followers recognized as a congregation for his archdiocese. He was willing to approach the office of the Propagation of the Faith in Rome for this recognition. But first a proposed constitution had to be drawn up.

It was decided that the new congregation should be called the Missionaries of Charity and that a fourth vow should be added to those of poverty, chastity, and obedience. It was *to give wholehearted and free service to the poorest of the poor."*

At a mass to celebrate the inauguration of the new congregation, Father Van Exem read out the decree of recognition. It stated,

"To fulfil our mission of compassion and love to the poorest of the
poor we go:
– seeking out in towns and villages all over the world even amid squalid
surroundings the poorest, the abandoned, the sick, the infirm, the leprosy
patients, the dying, the desperate, the lost, the outcasts,
– taking care of them,
– rendering help to them,
– visiting them assiduously,
– living Christ's love for them, and
– awakening their response to His great love."

It was on that day, October 7, 1950, and at that service that Sister Teresa became Mother Teresa, foundress of the Missionaries of Charity. Subashini Das was to become Sister Agnes, and Magdalena Gomes, Sister Gertrude.

As the community grew, so the upper room of the house in Creek Street became too small. Once again Father Van Exem, through his contacts in the city, was able to find a suitable property. It belonged to a Muslim who was about to move to Dacca. In February 1953, at a price that barely represented the value of the land it stood on, the diocese bought 54a Lower Circular Road. This became, and has remained to this day, the Mother House of the Missionaries of Charity. One room was converted into a chapel which served as a powerhouse for all their work with the poor, the sick, the homeless, and the dying. As Mother Teresa so firmly believes, without God her work is of little value and it is to God that all praise should be given for the achievements that are made. Like John the Baptist, she doesn't want to attract attention to herself. She has even said that, *"Facing the press is more difficult than bathing a leper."*[16] Her mission is that people should see Jesus. Her motive in agreeing to make a television program with Malcolm Muggeridge, an agreement which was not readily given, was so that, together, they could do *"something beautiful for God."*

Bringing beauty to the slums of Calcutta is not easy, but with God's help that was something Mother Teresa was determined to do. Among her priorities was the establishment of a home for the dying, as she firmly believed that: *"We cannot let a child of God die like an animal in the gutter."* [17] Kalighat is one of the most overcrowded parts of south Calcutta. It takes its name from a powerful Hindu goddess, Kali, whose ancient temple was on the banks of a tributary of the sacred river, the Ganges. It was here that Mother Teresa established her home for dying destitutes, Nirmal Hriday – Place of the Pure Heart, but not without difficulty.

Death was not something the orthodox Hindu found easy to cope with. It carried with it elements of impurity, so they, of necessity, kept their distance. Hindu landlords were not too happy to have tenants die in their property. Taxi or rickshaw drivers were not too willing to transport the terminally ill. And hospitals were not keen to admit patients for whom they knew they could do little medically. Moved by the sight of corpses dumped in the street and having prayed about the situation, Mother Teresa went to the Commissioner of Police and to the Health Officer of Calcutta to ask for a place where the destitute could die with dignity. She was given a pilgrims' hostel near the Temple of Kali. It was in a filthy condition but it had everything that was required: space, gas, and electricity. The sisters began to get it ready.

However, not all of the locals were quite so thrilled. They did not want these Christians working so close to their holy Hindu shrine. Rumors were circulating that people were being converted to Christianity. Complaints reached the ears of the Police Commissioner, who duly inspected Nirmal Hriday. He was impressed by what he saw and said to those who brought the complaint, *"I have said that I will get rid of this foreign lady and I will do so, but you must first get your mothers and your sisters to do what she is doing. In the Temple is a black stone image of the goddess Kali. But here, we have a living Kali!"*[18]

With a Christian community working on the very doorstep of a most sacred Hindu shrine there was bound to be tension. But the relationship between the Missionaries of Charity and the temple priests became far less tense after one of them was accepted by Mother Teresa into Nirmal Hriday. He was suffering from the last stages of tuberculosis and had been turned away by several Calcutta hospitals. He was given the same quality of care that everyone received, and gradually his tremendous resentment and anger against his illness changed. In his face there was acceptance and peace. And after they had realized that one of their fellow priests had been washed, fed, and comforted by people who asked for nothing in return, the priests of Kali became far less hostile.

The work with the dying is demanding and difficult. Both Mother Teresa and the Sisters knew that, in the majority of cases there was little that medical science could do. But that didn't stop them from offering the one experience which sustains people even on the point of death. The love Mother Teresa and the Sisters received from their faith in Jesus Christ they gave to all those who came within their care. And as the dying passed from this world to the next, Mother Teresa made sure that they were not alone.

Some people who often did find themselves alone and abandoned in Calcutta were the lepers. They were outcasts. Even those who came from well-to-do families would have to leave home so that the rest of the family wouldn't suffer because of their illness. Fathers left daughters for fear that no one would marry them. Sons would leave home for fear of bringing disgrace upon the family. Most lepers would carve out a meager existence by begging. As the disease took hold, they lost all sense of feeling and became susceptible to further infection and loss of limb.

In the television interview with Malcolm Muggeridge, Mother Teresa talked about her work with the lepers. The work started in 1957 with just five lepers who came to the Mother House. They had been thrown out of their work. Soon they were joined by a doctor, Dr. Senn, who not only treated the lepers but trained the Sisters for leprosy work. Much of this work was done through mobile clinics set up in the areas where the lepers gathered. The leper station was scheduled for the same hour at the same spot on the same day of each week. Records were kept, and if lepers were missing Mother Teresa and the Sisters would search the area until they were found.

The initiative taken by Mother Teresa meant that many more people became aware of the needs of the lepers. Various groups started collecting money by using an especially effective emblem. It was a bell, the traditional symbol of the unclean, surrounded by the motto, *"Touch the leper with your compassion."* The response was great. Not just from those who gave but from the lepers themselves. They now realized that they needn't be outcasts. Something could be done for their crippling illness.

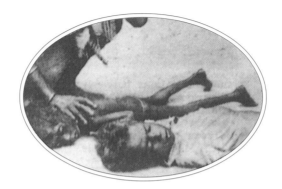

In 1969 the work with lepers came to fruition with the inauguration of a town for these people nobody wanted. The government had given Mother Teresa thirty-four acres of land, on which she built a town called Shanti Nagar, Town of Peace, where the lepers could live in peace. They were also accepted. Sister Francis Xavier, a Yugoslavian, was in charge of Shanti Nagar, and part of her work was to see that those lepers who had been cured received the rehabilitation treatment they needed to enable them to resume their place within society.

Malcolm Muggeridge's visit to Shanti Nagar with Mother Teresa made a very deep impression upon him. *"While I was walking with her, mixing with the crowd in the leper town, I constantly heard people mumbling the word 'mother.' It wasn't that they had anything to say to her, but simply that they wanted to establish a link with her."*[19]

"From my own point of view I went through three phases when I was among the lepers. The first was horror mixed with pity, the second compassion pure and simple, and the third reaching far beyond compassion, something I had never experienced before – an awareness that these dying and derelict men and women,

these lepers with stumps instead of hands, these unwanted children, were not pitiable, repulsive, or forlorn, but rather dear and delightful; as it might be friends of long standing, brothers, and sisters. How is it to be explained – the very heart and mystery of the Christian faith? To soothe those battered old heads, to grasp those poor stumps, to take in one's arms those children consigned to the dustbins, because it is His head, as they are His stumps and His children, of whom He said that whoever received one such child in His name received Him." [20]

It is her work with the children that has always been central to Mother Teresa's calling to serve the poorest of the poor. Nirmala Shishu Bhavan, the Children's Home of the Immaculate, became the center for this work. It is an unimposing two-story building with a large courtyard. There are children everywhere. But it is not only abandoned children who are cared for here, it also acts as the work center of the Missionaries of Charity, quite different from the cloistered serenity of the Mother House. When journalist Desmond Doig visited Shishu Bhavan he wrote, *"The tragedy of being abandoned, homeless, and unloved should pervade Shishu Bhavan, but it doesn't. There is a corner where unbelievably tiny infants are cared for, sometimes two or three to a cot, and often attached, as if*

still by their umbilical cords, to intravenous drip-feeders. There are infants picked up from the pavements, left on doorsteps, or outside police posts, in drains, or in refuse dumps. More recently, they have come also from city hospitals where Mother Teresa has left a standing request that all unwanted babies be handed over to her. 'I'm fighting abortion with adoption,' she says. I once had occasion to visit Shishu Bhavan on two consecutive days, and on the second day missed several wizened faces I remembered from the day before. I asked a Sister attending where they were. She said they had died; they had not had a chance really. So many of them died, but it was better that they died here, where they were cared for, and where love battled to keep them alive."[21]

Mother Teresa's work with the dying, the lepers, and the children, with the poorest of the poor, has spread from its humble beginnings in Calcutta to many places throughout the world. In places as far apart as Melbourne and London, Rome and New York, Peru and Manila the work of the Missionaries of Charity was established. And it was not just work centers that were established. Houses for the training of the novitiate began to spring up around the world as more people wished to test their vocation to join Mother Teresa in creating something beautiful for God. The community had also grown in other ways. In 1963 the Missionaries of Charity Brothers were founded. Priests like Father Van Exem and Father Henry had been a tremendous help to Mother Teresa in the early days but there was now a definite need for a group of men who would work in the same spirit as the Sisters. The initial group consisted of a priest and twelve young men anxious to commit their lives to working among the poor. They lived on the first floor of Shishu Bhavan.

A young Jesuit priest, Father Ian Travers-Ball left his homeland, Australia, and arrived in India in 1954. In 1963 he was ordained as a Jesuit priest, and two years later he got permission to spent a month living with the Brothers, founded by Mother Teresa. It was to be in the nature of an experiment so that he could see how he could serve the poor as a Jesuit. He joined the group who were living at Shishu Bhavan and experienced at first hand the work that was being done.

The spiritual supervision of the Brothers was in the hands of Father Henry, when he could spare the time from his other duties, and in those of Mother Teresa. But this could only be a temporary arrangement, partly because the Catholic Church does not permit a woman to be the head of a male congregation. Father Travers-Ball was deeply moved both by the poverty and simplicity of the Brothers and the way in which they carried out their work. He also realized their need for a priest to be with them full time to help them with their spiritual growth.

At the end of the trial month Mother Teresa, who is never one to miss an opportunity, asked Father Travers-Ball if he would stay and become the head of the male congregation. He agreed, providing his Jesuit superiors would give him permission. In January 1966 he received a letter from the superior general of the Society of Jesus in Rome which gave him three options, the third of which was to make a complete break with the Jesuit order and join the male branch of the Missionaries of Charity. So like Mother Teresa he left his first call and accepted the call within a call to serve the poor of the world. He became the male founder of the Missionaries of Charity Brothers, chose the title of General Servant and the name, Brother Andrew. Mother Teresa once remarked of Brother Andrew, *"We are so different, but both of us have the same mind."*[22]

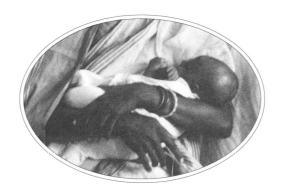

Mother Teresa and Brother Andrew were not the only people to be of the same mind. In 1954 Ann Blaikie, the wife of a British businessman working in India contacted Mother Teresa with an offer to make toys for the children's Christmas party. The offer was accepted, but instead of toys, Mother Teresa wanted dresses, shirts, and pants for the children. Clothes then needed to be made so that they could be given to the children to celebrate Muslim and Hindu festivals. What might have been seen as a one-time offer of help was turned by Mother Teresa into an act of real commitment.

The strength of support grew, and the volunteers, as well as working with the children, the lepers, and the dying, found themselves spending time with the young Sisters teaching them English, the language of the congregation. As always, the demands that Mother Teresa made were great. One day when Ann Blaikie sent a message that she would not be able to accompany her because she had a fever, Mother Teresa remarked, *"I also have a fever, but it is better to burn in this world than in the next."*[23]

Interest in the work of Mother Teresa and the Missionaries of Charity spread throughout the world. But Mother Teresa made it clear that it wasn't just financial support that they wanted. What she had in mind was the formation of a spiritual family which shared her vision for the work that she was doing. It was to be like the Third Order of St. Francis, which allowed lay people to follow the spiritual path of St. Francis without committing themselves to the life-binding vows of the Order.

In 1969 Mother Teresa drew up, with the help of others, the regulations for the International Association of the Co-Workers of Mother Teresa and on March 26, as Head of the Society, she presented them to His Holiness Pope Paul VI. There was one thing, though, that was rather special about the Co-Workers. It states in the first paragraph of the regulations, *"The International Association of Co-Workers of Mother Teresa consists of men, women, young people, and children of all religions and denominations throughout the world, who seek to love God in their fellow men, through wholehearted service to the poorest of the poor of all castes and creeds, and who wish to unite themselves in a spirit of prayer and sacrifice with the work of Mother Teresa and the Missionaries of Charity."*

It was not only the physically fit who were able to become Co-Workers. A Belgian, Jacqueline de Decker, had served as a nurse in Antwerp during World War II, and, on December 31, 1946 she realized her ambition and set sail to work in India. During her visit to Patna she met Mother Teresa, who told her that she wanted to remain a nun and hoped to have companions.

Jacqueline wanted to work with her, but before she could she had to return to Belgium for medical treatment.

During her stay in Belgium, she developed a paralysis that affected an arm, an eye, and a leg. Then followed 20 operations on her spine. Her chances of returning to work with Mother Teresa in India were negligible. She wrote to Mother Teresa, who realized the practical difficulties of Jacqueline working with the poorest of the poor, but that didn't mean that Mother Teresa thought that Jacqueline had nothing to offer. She suggested that, from her home in Belgium, Jacqueline could support the work that was being done in India through her own suffering and her prayers. And so was born the Sick and Suffering Co-Workers of Mother Teresa, who link themselves to the suffering of others through prayer and their own pain.

With a team of Sisters, Brothers, and Co-Workers, Mother Teresa endeavored to respond to the ever-growing demands of the poorest of the poor. People throughout the world came to recognize this small woman, in her simple white sari with a blue border and a small black crucifix pinned to it, as a source for the powerless and a voice for those who had no voice. Awards were showered upon her for the work that she did. 1971 alone saw her receive the Pope John XXIII Peace Prize from Pope Paul VI, The Good Samaritan Award of the National Catholic Development Conference in Boston, Massachusetts, and an honorary doctorate of Humane Letters at the Catholic University of America in Washington, D.C. At the last moment, Mother Teresa was unable to receive the last two awards in person. At the time she was facing a very large problem with refugees, and their needs came first.

She did however manage to get to the United States later in 1971 to receive an award from the Joseph P. Kennedy Jr. Foundation. After stopping in Rome and Belfast, she was greeted with great love and excitement by the Sisters

on her arrival in New York. When Senator Edward Kennedy made the presentation to Mother Teresa he said, *"In her unique geography of compassion, Mother Teresa knows where the need is, and in her unique faith never doubts that the means to meet it, in help and material resources, will be forthcoming. It is our privilege to ensure that her faith is ever more abundantly fulfilled."*[24]

Following her visit to the States, she went to Toronto to speak on the subject of the "Secret of Peace" with Jean Vanier, the Founder of the L'Arche Movement, a movement which cares especially for those who have a mental disability. From Toronto it was back to New York and a television appearance with Malcolm Muggeridge whose program, *"Something Beautiful for God"* had just been released. The interviewer was David Frost. His questioning concentrated on the problem of suffering as against the idea of a loving God. But Mother Teresa simply summed up her work by saying, *"You must know the poor in order to love them. You must love the poor in order to serve them."*[25]

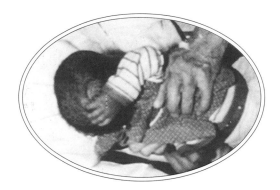

Awards continued to come thick and fast, despite Mother Teresa's reticence to draw attention to herself. She firmly believes that the work she is doing is the work that she has been called by God to do. And it is from God that she receives the strength to do it. At the very heart of her work is her devotion to God, her regular reception of the Blessed Sacrament in the Mass, and her daily devotions. Without this discipline Mother Teresa wouldn't be able to function. And she makes the same demands on her Sisters. They, too, must be faithful in prayer and regular at Mass. This is their first priority despite the constant daily demands of caring for the poorest of the poor.

Mother Teresa has never involved herself or her Sisters in the work of fundraising. She has always believed that as the work is of God then He will make sure that the necessary funds are made available. After all, she started out with only five rupees, and that in no way limited the response that she was able to make to God's call. At times there has been an extra bonus. As when Pope Paul VI, who was attending the 1964 Eucharistic Congress in Bombay, gave her a white Cadillac car which had been a gift to him from Notre Dame University in Indiana. She decided to raffle it and raised 460,000 rupees for her work.

In 1973 Mother Teresa was the first recipient of the Templeton Prize for Progress in Religion. Out of over 2,000 nominations, the nine judges, who were drawn from the major religious traditions of the world, chose Mother Teresa. The citation read, *"She has been instrumental in widening and deepening man's knowledge and love of God and thereby furthering the quest for the quality of life that mirrors the divine."*[26] And Prince Philip, when he presented the award to Mother Teresa in London's Guildhall said, *"Mother Teresa has shown by her life what people can do when the faith is strong. By any standard what she has done is good, and the world today is desperately in need of this sort of goodness, this sort of practical compassion."*[27]

This was not to be the only "first" she received. In 1975 she was the first recipient of the Albert Schweitzer International Prize in recognition of her "reverence for life." But the award that really attracted the attention of the world was the Nobel Peace Prize. Mother Teresa had been nominated for it four years earlier, but on that occasion it was awarded to Andrei Sakharov. However, in 1979 in the Aula Magna of the University of Oslo, she was to receive this one of

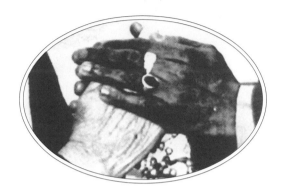

the world's most prestigious awards because as was stated, *"Mother Teresa works in the world as she finds it, in the slums of Calcutta and other towns and cities. But she makes no distinction between poor and rich persons, between poor and rich countries."*[28] As always she received these awards with utter humility and the substantial sums of money that she received from these awards were used in the furtherance of her work.

Mother Teresa's work continued to focus on meeting the needs of the poor, but the leaders of the world were anxious to meet her and hear at first hand about that work. The American President Ronald Reagan invited her to a lunch at The White House. Pope John Paul II asked her, in 1982, to visit war torn Lebanon as his envoy. She managed to rescue 37 mentally handicapped children from a bombed hospital. Russian President Mikhail Gorbachov readily accepted her offer of help, and so began the Missionaries of Charity work in Albania and other Eastern European countries.

In 1980 Prince Charles made a special journey to her mission in Calcutta during a tour of India. On a subsequent tour with his wife in 1992 a

proposed meeting was postponed because of Mother Teresa's poor health. On returning to London Princess Diana made a special journey to Rome where Mother Teresa was convalescing. The fragile nun and the glamorous Princess spent time in conversation and prayer.

Whenever she has met political leaders she has never been afraid to make them face up to the problems on their own doorstep, as she did with the British Premier Margaret Thatcher on the subject of housing and with President Reagan on nuclear arms. And her opposition to abortion is total.

Mother Teresa has her critics. Australian author Germaine Greer sees her as a "religious imperialist," believing that the relief of human distress should be undertaken for its own sake and not as a way of forcing a creed on people who are especially vulnerable. In a particularly hard-hitting newspaper article, she wrote, *"Mother Teresa epitomises for me the blinkered charitableness upon which we pride ourselves and for which we expect reward in this world and the next."*[29]

Underlying everything that Mother Teresa does is her faith in God. Her prayers and devotions come first and it is upon God that she depends totally for everything. A former secretary to the Archbishop of Westminster in England, Cardinal Hume, recalls how Mother Teresa would sometimes withdraw into a quiet and secret world of her own for spiritual refreshment. *"It was as if she had some inner chamber where she could go."*[30]

In April 1990 Mother Teresa announced that she was stepping down as Superior of her Order for health reasons. Her followers, however, refused to accept her resignation, and re-elected her as their leader in September. She agreed to carry on.

The rest of the story can now only be told in pictures, for the world of Mother Teresa is at least as visual as it is anything else. It can be absorbed truly only by the direct experience of seeing her at work. However, the following pages come as close as we can manage, and the hope is that readers will find a taste herein of one of the greatest individuals of this century.

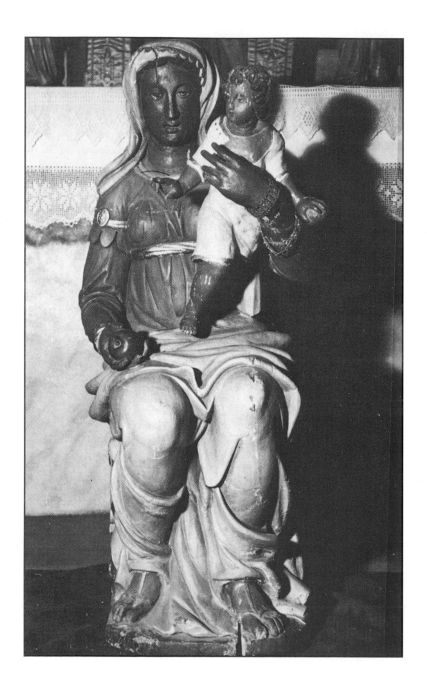

*The statue of the Madonna of Letnice. The Bojaxhiu family made the
pilgrimage to the shrine in Letnice every year.*

THE EARLY YEARS IN SKOPJE

Opposite page, far left: *The young Mother Teresa – Agnes Gonxha Bojaxhiu – as a child taking part in a Christmas Eve play performed at her primary school in Skopje, Yugoslavia.* Right: *Agnes with two friends in Skopje.* Below: *Agnes with other pupils at the school of the Sacred Heart in Skopje.* This page, right: *Agnes (right) with her brother Lazar and sister Aga, 1924.* Below: *Agnes and her sister Aga (holding the parasol) on a trip to Nerezima with friends.*

Agnes in 1928, shortly before she left for Ireland.

THE LONG AWAITED ARRIVAL IN INDIA

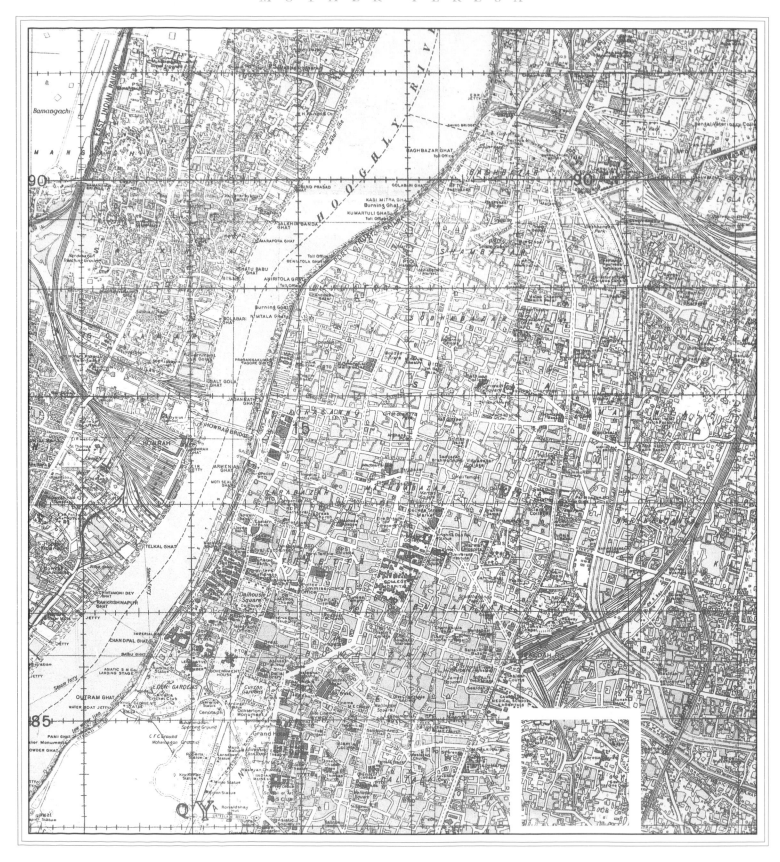

In the late 1920s, when young Gonxha first arrived in Calcutta, one of the main river crossings was the Howrah floating bridge, which now no longer exists.

An old map showing the city of Calcutta and in particular the area in which the Loreto convent is situated.

Above: *View of the Hooghly river from Calcutta in the late 1920s. It is here that the ship bringing Gonxha to India docked.* Opposite page: *The Calcutta docks are today a sign of India's fast race towards industrialization. The view now is very different from the time when Mother Teresa arrived in the city as a young girl.*

Above: *A picture of Chowringhee, a prosperous area in Calcutta, where merchants and whining beggars rubbed shoulders surrounded by filth.* Below: *A view of Calcutta at the time of the British Raj.*

HOME AWAY FROM HOME; THE LORETO CONVENT

Left: *Sister Teresa (left) as a novice in Darjeeling in 1929. This was the first photograph received by her family from India.* Above and right: *The Loreto convent in Darjeeling lies in an idyllic position, high up on the hills and surrounded by the magnificent Himalayan range, which is believed by the Hindus to be the heavenly abode of Shiva. This is where young Agnes Gonhxa Bojaxhiu was first sent to improve her English and to become familiar with the strict discipline of convent life.*

Top left: *The Loreto convent in Darjeeling provided a day school for local girls. This old photograph, reproduced from the album of the Loreto Sisters, shows girl pupils playing badminton with their nun teacher during games. Young Sister Teresa was their English teacher at the time.* Top right: *The Mother Superior of the Loreto convent is seen here with guests in 1936 within the convent's compound.* Bottom left: *A view of the tea plantations on the hillside surrounding the city taken in the 1930s.* Bottom right: *The city's main square, Chowrasta, at the time of the British Raj. The local social scene provided a strong contrast to the lives of the Loreto Sisters who were not allowed outside the convent walls.*

The full visual impact of the Himalayan range can be seen from the hills surrounding Darjeeling. One can make out the basket bearers and helpers for an unusual outing of the Loreto Sisters. The Sisters are predominantly Irish. Here we see them at the time when Sister Teresa lived in the convent having a picnic on the hills surrounding Darjeeling.

Assembly Hall in the Loreto School. On the right we can see Sister Francis Michael who was a novice with Sister Teresa and remembers that she was known

*then as "our little Yugoslav postulant." She says that "she was hard-working, zealous, she prayed
hard and didn't seem exceptional at the time."*

School girls during a break in the grounds of the convent

. . . and eating their lunch.

Top left: *The chapel of Loreto is the focal point of the Sisters' daily activities for they gather here to pray several times a day.* Top right: *Sister Teresa and Sister Francis Michael having a picnic.*
Bottom left: *The feast of All Saints celebrated in the garden of the Loreto convent in 1933.*
Bottom right: *Luscious and dense forests enclose Darjeeling providing then, as they do now, ample opportunity for solitary wanderings.*

LORETO ENTALLY, CALCUTTA; THE VOCATION EXPANDS

Loreto Entally, as the convent of the Loreto Sisters is commonly known in Calcutta, was one of the first centers of missionary activity available to European nuns in India. From Darjeeling, where she learned English and Hindi, Sister Teresa was sent to Calcutta where she enjoyed her work as a teacher in the school for local day pupils.
Here we see the entrance gate of Loreto Entally.

Life at Loreto Entally followed the same strict discipline as in Darjeeling. The Sisters were never allowed out, and thus knew little or nothing of what was happening on the other side of the compound walls in the Indian world. India, under the rule of the British Raj, was suffering and seeking a new role for itself in the fabric of history.

Opposite page, top: *Sister Teresa (right) after taking her first vows, May 23, 1929 at the Loreto convent in Entally, Calcutta.* Below: *Girl pupils during physical education class on the grounds of Loreto Entally in 1936.* Above: *View of the Loreto Sisters' quarters in Calcutta. This is where Sister Teresa came in 1937 after taking lifetime vows of poverty, chastity, and obedience in Darjeeling. Loreto Entally became her home and she is said to state that leaving Loreto was the most difficult task in the world.*

The Entally cloisters today.

Sister Eileen, the Mother Superior of Loreto Entally. She knows Mother from the time when they lived together in Loreto. Referring to Mother Teresa she says "She deserves the attention she gets. She has set an example. Of course, it is really a tribute to the fortitude of the poor people she is assisting. Now the sisters here have moved outside these walls; it is impossible to ask them (the pupils) to be punctual if you have not visited the families and realized that twenty people are sharing the same tap."

MALADMINISTRATION IN BENGAL   19

IN CALCUTTA—OCT. 24, '43

Above: Death at the crossways (Harrison Road, Strand Road). Left—Family of three beside shrouded corpse of fourth member—the father.

Undernourished children tend infant while mother seeks food.

Happier sight: Mealtime, at a Government feeding centre.

Mourning mother and dead child.

Left—Mother tending two moribund children. Above—One child dead; mother feeds the survivor.

A young mother, with a child clasped to her breast, weak from want of food, lies on the pavement of a Calcutta street, while a man, apparently on the verge of death, is in the background. Right.—H. E. Sir Thomas Rutherford made an informal daylight tour of relief centres in the Calcutta area in mid-September.

A great famine hit Bengal in 1943 – all rice and other food deliveries were stopped and people starved. Sister Teresa was driven out into the streets of Calcutta, despite the rules set by the convent, in search of something to eat to bring back to the pupils at the school where she taught. Having lived in the seclusion of the Loreto convent, venturing out into the streets strewn with the dead and dying was an eye-opening experience for the young nun. This is a page from The Statesman, *a popular British newspaper of the time.*

THE GREAT FAMINE
AND
DIRECT ACTION DAY

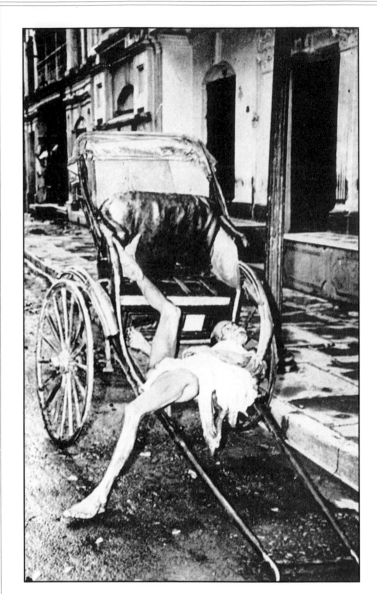

Right: *In 1946 another disaster struck Calcutta: in the Hindu-Muslim conflict that preceded the partitioning and the freedom of India, a "Direct Action Day" was declared by the Muslim League for August 16. The day was declared a holiday by the Muslim leader of Calcutta three days before Direct Action Day. With people free from work and Muslims at white heat over partitioning a mass meeting was called by the Muslim League on the Maidan, one of Calcutta's parks. As the meeting broke up, Direct Action Day exploded into a fury of blood and violence. This photograph shows the carnage following the rioting in 1946.* Left: *The streets were brought to a standstill and the city was gripped by horror and violence. Some 6,000 people lost their lives in the riots.*

As a result of the rioting and carnage all food deliveries were stopped and as headmistress of the school Sister Teresa had to take action. "I went out from St. Mary's, Entally" she related, "I had three hundred girls in the boarding school and we had nothing to eat."

The round table conference during which ideas of freeing India from the British Government's grip were discussed.

Left: *Prime Minister Nehru, May 1946.* Right: *India led by Gandhi and his nonviolent movement was searching for a new identity and freedom. Here is Gandhi after the first interview in 1946.*

Howrah station in Calcutta.

THE CALL
WITHIN A CALL

Left: *Howrah station, the departure point to Darjeeling in the 1920s. It was from here that Sister Teresa left Entally to go to Darjeeling for her annual retreat after her disturbing foray into the streets of a city bloodied by massacre.* Above: *Carriage interior.* Below: *Porters at Howrah station.*

Above: *It was on the long train journey from Calcutta to Darjeeling that Sister Teresa received a revelation. "I was going to Darjeeling to make my retreat," she explains. "It was on that train that I heard the call to give up all and follow Him into the slums, to serve Him in the poorest of the poor. I knew that it was His will and that I had to follow Him. There was no doubt that it was to be His work." The narrow gauge steam train that took passengers to Darjeeling in the 1940s. Right: This photograph shows the "agony loop," a characteristic system which helped trains on the steep inclines on their journey to Darjeeling.*

Darjeeling.

Darjeeling.

A statue of the Virgin Mary stands over the entrance of the Mother House in Calcutta.

THE FIRST TRUE HOME; MOTHER HOUSE

Above: *Sisters of Charity hanging their saris to dry.*
Right: *Mother Teresa talks with a Sister of Charity.*
Throughout the headquarters there are reminders, quotes from
the Bible, and notes painted on the walls.

Above: *An icon of a madonna with child dominates the otherwise bare space. The Mother House is the central headquarters of the world-wide network of the Missionaries of Charity. Left: The decree of recognition of the Order founded by Mother Teresa states that the Missionaries of Charity seek in towns and villages the poorest, the abandoned, the sick, the infirm, the leprosy patients, the dying, the desperate, the lost, the outcasts. The daily work of the Missionaries is thus conducted in the streets and slums where they provide a constant source of help.*

Mother Teresa driving in an ambulance to provide help.

Two Sisters of Charity in the market.

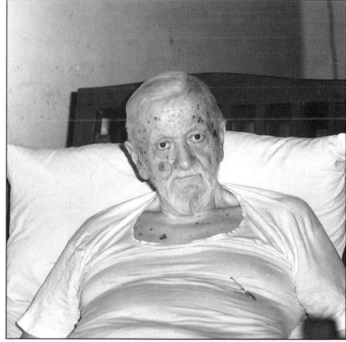

Mother Teresa with members of her Order, the Missionaries of Charity. Directly above: Father Celeste Van Exem SJ, Mother's spiritual guide for many years.

"I am fighting abortion with adoption."

SHISHU BHAVAN –
CHILDREN'S HOME
FOR THE BLIND, DUMB,
CRIPPLED AND ABANDONED

Sisters of Charity visiting a family.

The entrance to Shishu Bhavan, the home for children. It is Mother Teresa's work with the children that has always been central to her calling to serve the poorest of the poor. The Hindi name literally means Children's Home of the Immaculate: here tiny infants, abandoned by their mothers, as well as older children are cared for.

Left: *Mother Teresa in Shishu Bhavan. Many of the children who are welcomed here are blind, dumb, crippled, or simply abandoned.* Above: *Mother Teresa in the nursery.*

Stall selling Hindu souvenirs by Kalighat.

NIRMAL HRIDAY – THE PLACE OF THE PURE HEART, HOME FOR THE DYING DESTITUTES

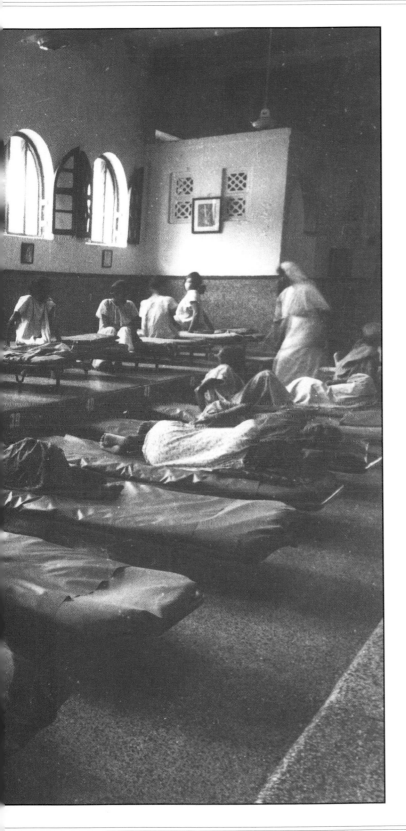

Left: *The Women's Ward of the Home for the Dying Destitutes.* Above: *Nirmal Hriday, the Place of the Pure Heart and Home for the Dying Destitutes, is in very close proximity to Kalighat, one of the holiest Hindu shrines in India, on the banks of a tributary of the sacred river, the Ganges. The temple is dedicated to the powerful Goddess Kali, to whom in the past the priests of the temple used to offer sacrifices of small animals. The inner sanctum of the temple is stained with blood. To establish a home for the dying opposite the temple was, to say the least, a very controversial step. Here we see the Kalighat temple in 1931.*

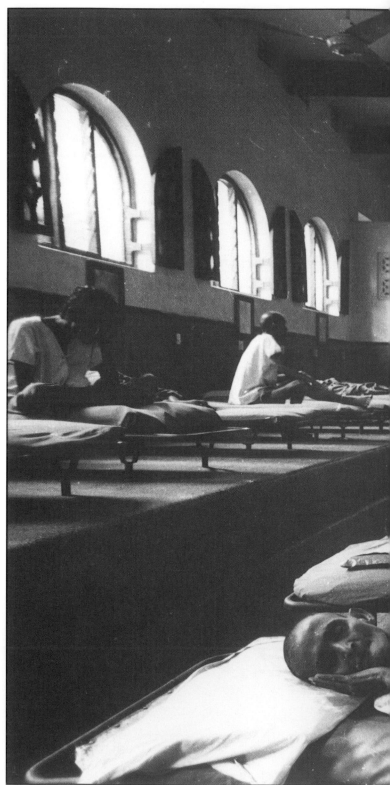

Right: *The Men's Ward*. Above: *The Washroom of the Home for the Dying*.

This poem has been written on one of the walls of Nirmal Hriday:

"*If you have two pieces of bread*
Give one to the poor
Sell the other
And buy hyacinths
To feed your soul."

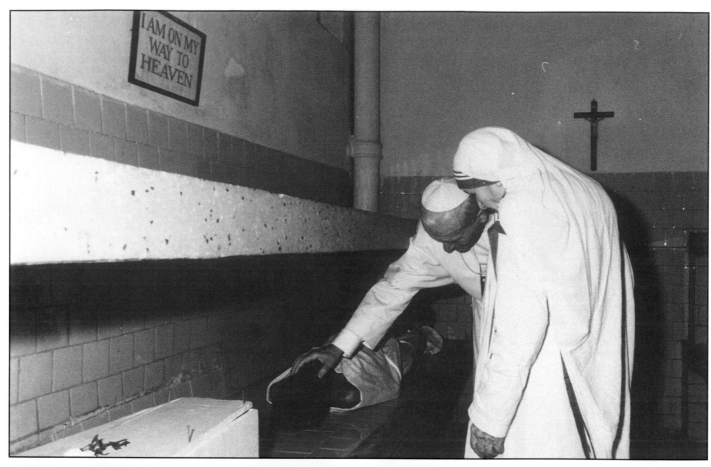

Above: *Sisters of Charity in an ambulance outside Kalighat. Every day they venture into the slums looking for those in need.* Opposite page, top: *Pope John Paul II visited Nirmal Hriday in 1986.* Bottom left: *Women's Ward.* Right: *The common room of the "death row" where Mother Teresa welcomes all and provides nourishment both to the spirit and to the body.*

Homeless sleeping in the streets of Calcutta.

सिटिजेन वाच
CHOWK BA

Sisters of Charity.

The shanty town of the untouchables.

John Sanness, Chairman of Norway's Nobel Committee, presents the Nobel Peace Prize during the awards ceremony in Oslo, December 10, 1979.

MOTHER TERESA RECEIVES THE WORLD'S RECOGNITION FOR HER WORK

Left: *Mother Teresa climbing the steps to the Aula Magna of the University of Oslo, Norway, where she received the Nobel Peace Prize in 1979.* Above: *Two Nobel Prize winners: Mother Teresa with Archbishop Desmond Tutu in South Africa in 1988.*

Right: *Mother Teresa with Edward Kennedy whilst visiting a refugee camp in Bangladesh.* Above: *Sisters of Charity in mission.*

Right: *President and Mrs. Ronald Reagan escort Mother Teresa from The White House after her visit there. Behind them is Sister Priscilla, Mother's aide.* Above: *With Indian Prime Minister Indira Gandhi, in 1980.*

Above: *Palestine Liberation Organization Chairman, Yasser Arafat, visits Calcutta and presents Mother with a check for $50,000 for the work of the Missionaries of Charity in 1990.*
Right: *With French President Giscard d'Estaing. She spoke to him of her project to open an establishment of her order, the Missionaries of Charity, in Marseilles, France.*

Mother is awarded her adopted country's highest civilian award,
The Jewel of India (the Bharat Ratna).

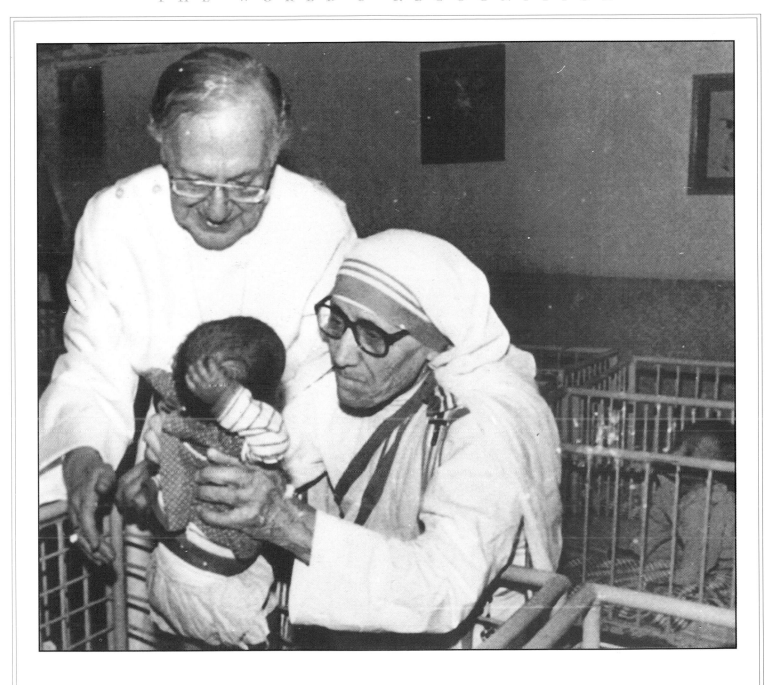

With the Archbishop of Canterbury – Dr. A.K. Runcie – visiting.

Left: *Visiting children at the Sabra psychiatric hospital in Beirut West.*

Mother Teresa with John Paul II.

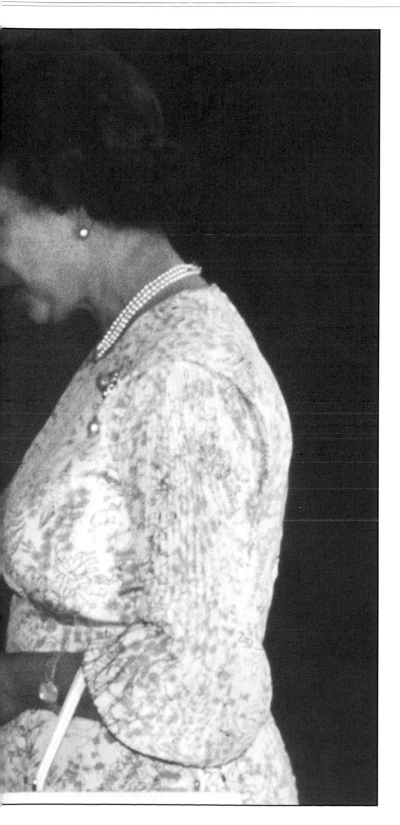

Above: *Princess Diana holds the hands of Mother Teresa during their meeting at the convent where Mother is staying after being released from the clinic following a bout of pneumonia and heart problems in 1992.* Left: *Queen Elizabeth II meets Mother in Delhi and presents her with the Insignia of the Honorary Order of Merit in 1983.*

Celebrating mass.

Receiving communion.

Addressing a conference for human rights.

Above: *Mother Teresa and two of her Missionaries of Charity.*
Left: *At The White House with George and Barbara Bush.*

The Loreto convent grounds.

Whilst every effort has been made to trace all present copyright holders of this material, whether companies or individuals, any unintentional omission is hereby apologized for in advance and we will be pleased to correct any errors in acknowledgments in any future edition of this book.

Front cover © Frank Spooner Pictures, London

Back Cover © Simon Weinstock, London

The publishers would like to thank the following contributors to the book.

The Royal Commonwealth Society for letting us browse through their very extensive and unique photographic collection which covers two centuries of events. We are especially grateful to them for letting us reproduce some archive material in this book.

Das Studio of Darjeeling for giving us access to some wonderful period photography of the city in the 1920s and 30s.

The Loreto Sisters in Darjeeling who opened the gates of their convent to our intrepid photographer Gary Woods and welcomed him, allowing us to reproduce pictures taken from their own collection.

The Loreto Sisters in Entally, Calcutta, who found the time to talk to our photographer and allowed him to take pictures within the Entally compound.

Father Celeste Van Exem who, despite being unwell, welcomed Gary Woods and talked to him.

The British Library India House for all their help and collaboration.

Georges Gorree and Jean Barbier Malcolm Muggeridge, David Porter, Eileen Egan, Geoffrey Moorhouse, and Desmond Doig for the use of material from their books.

And, finally, Gary Woods for taking off to India at such short notice and returning to us with such a wonderful document.

Acknowledgments

The publishers and the authors wish to thank the following for allowing reproduction of their photographs and maps in the present work:

Drita Publishing, @ Editrice Velar Spa, 1992: 52, top left 54, 55. Dott. don Lush Gjergji: bottom 54, top right 54, 56, 64, top 76, 151. Labyrinth Publishing photographic archive: 57, 82. Map Collection of Calcutta 1929, India House, British Library, London: 58. Photographic Collection, India House, British Library, London: 84, 85, 88/9, 90/1. *"Port of Calcutta 1870-1920"*, the Calcutta Port Trust, Thacker, Spink and Co., Calcutta and Simla, 1920: 60. *"Calcutta"* by G.W. Tyson, 1931: 59, 115. Gary Woods, London: 61, 65, 68/9, 70/1, top left 72, 74, 75, 77, 78, 79, 86, 89, bottom 90, 94, top 96, 99, 101, 103, 106, 107, 111, 112, 119, 120, 122/3, 124, 125, 126/7, 132, 154. *"Recollections of Calcutta for over Half a Century"* M. Massey; Thacker, Spink and Co., Calcutta 1918. Photo by Bourne and Shepherd: 62. Extracts from *"The Statesman"* 1945, p. 2 – Filthy Calcutta: The Empire's Second City: 62. – Maladministration in Bengal: 80. Das Studio, Darjeeling: 66, 72. Loreto Sisters, Darjeeling: 67. *"First the Blade"*, Mother Mary Colmcille: bottom 76. *"The Last Days of the British Raj"*, Leonard Mosley; Weidenfeld and Nicholson, London, 1961: left 82. *"The Last Days of the Raj"*, Trevor Royce; Michael Joseph, London, 1989: 83. Indian Railways Board, 1940: top 90. Frank Spooner Pictures, London: 96/7, 98, 100, 102/3, 104, 108, 116, 118, 130, 132/3, 136/7, 140/1, 142, 143, 146, 148/9, 150/1. Associated Press, London: 6, 109, 128, 131, 134, 135, 136, 138, 139, 144/5, 147, 149, Syndication International Ltd, London: 51, 110, 141, 147, 152, 153. K. Polkowski, 1992: 114/5, 116/7, bottom left 118, top 116.

Bibliographical References

1. *Mother Teresa – The Early Years*, David Porter, SPCK, London, 1977.

2. *Something Beautiful For God*, Malcolm Muggeridge, Harper & Row, San Francisco, 1977; Fount Paperbacks, an imprint of HarperCollinsPublishers Ltd., London, 1977.

3. Ibid.

4. *Such a Vision of the Street*, Eileen Egan, Sidgwick & Jackson, London, 1985.

5. *India Brittanica*, Geoffrey Moorhouse, Grafton Books, London, 1984.

6. *Such a Vision of the Street*, Eileen Egan, Sidgwick & Jackson, London, 1985.

7. Ibid.

8. *Mother Teresa – The Early Years*, David Porter, SPCK, London, 1977.

9. *Such a Vision of the Street*, Eileen Egan, Sidgwick & Jackson, London, 1985.

10. Ibid.

11. Ibid.

12. Ibid.

13. Ibid.

14. Ibid.

15. *Mother Teresa – The Early Years*, David Porter, SPCK, London, 1986.

16. *You* Magazine, April 19th 1992.

17. *Such a Vision of the Street*, Eileen Egan, Sidgwick & Jackson, London, 1985.

18. *Mother Teresa – The Early Years*, David Porter, SPCK, London, 1986.

19. *For the Love of God*, Georges Gorree and Jean Barbier, Veritas Publications, Dublin, Ireland, 1974.

20. Ibid.

21. *Mother Teresa – Her People and her Work*, Desmond Doig, Harper & Row, San Francisco, 1980; Fount Paperbacks, an imprint of HarperCollinsPublishers Ltd., London, 1978.

22. *Such a Vision of the Street*, Eileen Egan, Sidgwick & Jackson, London, 1985.

23. Ibid.

24. Ibid.

25. Ibid.

26. Ibid.

27. Ibid.

28. Ibid.

29. *The Independent*, Germaine Greer, September 22nd 1990.

30. *The Observer*, August 26th 1990.